Nutty *Knock Knocks*

by Karen Markoe & Louis Phillips
Illustrated by David Gantz

Wanderer Books
Published by Simon & Schuster, New York

Designed by Irving Grunbaum
Manufactured in the United States of America
10 9 8 7 6 5 4 3 2 1

WANDERER and colophon are trademarks of Simon & Schuster

FUNNYBONES is a trademark of Simon & Schuster

Library of Congress Cataloging in Publication Data

Markoe, Karen.
Nutty Knock Knocks.

(Funnybones)
SUMMARY: Contains a collection of knock-knock jokes.
1. Knock-knock jokes.   2. Wit and humor, Juvenile.
[1. Knock-knock jokes.   2. Jokes]   I. Phillips, Louis,
joint author.   II. Gantz, David.   III. Title.
PN6231.K55M3   1981   818'.5407   80-24328
ISBN 0-671-42249-9

Knock, Knock.
Who's there?
Nose.
Nose who?
I nose some more Knock-Knock jokes.

Knock, Knock.
Who's there?
Ears.
Ears who?
Ears some more Knock-Knock jokes for you.

Knock, Knock.
Who's there?
Chin.
Chin who?
Chin up. I'm not going to tell you any more
Knock-Knocks.

Knock, Knock.
Who's there?
Eisenhower.
Eisenhower who?
Eisenhower late for supper.

Knock, Knock.
Who's there?
Luke.
Luke who?
Luke and see who it is.

Knock, Knock.
Who's there?
Element.
Element who?
Element to tell you that she can't see you today.

Knock, Knock.
Who's there?
Dozen.
Dozen who?

Knock, Knock.
Who's there?
Tyrone.
Tyrone who?
Tyrone shoelaces, you're old enough.

Knock, Knock.
Who's there?
Ooze.
Ooze who?
Ooze in charge here?

Knock, Knock.
Who's there?
Dinosaur.
Dinosaur who?
Dinosaur because you called her stupid.

Knock, Knock.
Who's there?
Says.
Says who?
Says me, that's who.

Knock, Knock.
Who's there?
Holmes.
Holmes who?
Holmes is where the heart is.

Knock, Knock.
Who's there?
Watson.
Watson who?
Watson your mind?

Knock, Knock.
Who's there?
Turnip.
Turnip who?

Knock, Knock.
Who's there?
Oscar.
Oscar who?
Oscar silly question and you get a silly answer.

Knock, Knock.
Who's there?
Eileen.
Eileen who?
Eileen over backwards to make a compromise.

Knock, Knock.
Who's there?
Harmony.
Harmony who?
Harmony Knock-Knock jokes do you expect me to know?

Knock, Knock.
Who's there?
Ice cream.
Ice cream who?
Ice cream if you don't let me in.

Knock, Knock.
Who's there?
July.
July who?
July to me about who stole my pencil?

Knock, Knock.
Who's there?
Tank.
Tank who?
You're welcome.

Knock, Knock.
Who's there?
Doughnut.
Doughnut who?

Knock, Knock.
Who's there?
Hominy.
Hominy who?
Hominy people living in this house?

Knock, Knock.
Who's there?
Scold.
Scold who?
Scold enough to go ice-skating, isn't it?

Knock, Knock.
Who's there?
Ida.
Ida who?
It's not Ida who, it's Idaho.

Knock, Knock.
Who's there?
Cash.
Cash who?
I didn't realize you were some kind of nut.

Knock, Knock.
Who's there?
Adam.
Adam who?
Adam up and tell me the total.

Knock, Knock.
Who's there?
Sincerely.
Sincerely who?
Sincerely in the morning I have been waiting for you to open the door.

Knock, Knock.
Who's there?
Who.
Who who?

Knock, Knock.
Who's there?
Joe. *Will you remember my name?*
Certainly.
Will you remember me tomorrow?
Of course.
Will you remember me next week?
Yes.
Will you remember me in a month?
Yes.
Will you remember me next year?
Yes.

Knock, Knock.
Who's there?
See! You forgot already.

Knock, Knock.
Who's there?
Athena.
Athena who?
Athena reindeer landing on your roof.

Knock, Knock.
Who's there?
Alpaca.
Alpaca who?
Alpaca the car, you get the kids.

Knock, Knock.
Who's there?
Old King Cole.
Old King Cole who?
Old King Cole, so turn up the heat.

Knock, Knock.
Who's there?
Cheyenne.
Cheyenne who?
Cheyenne is too bashful to answer you herself.

Knock, Knock.
Who's there?
Weasel.
Weasel who?

Knock, Knock.
Who's there?
Tabasco.
Tabasco who?
Tabasco sauce. Isn't that a hot one?

Knock, Knock.
Who's there?
Kentucky.
Kentucky who?
Kentucky come out to play?

Knock, Knock.
Who's there?
Bucky Dent.
Bucky Dent who?
Bucky Dent the new automobile on the way
over here.

Knock, Knock.
Who's there?
Hammond.
Hammond who?
Hammond eggs.

Knock, Knock.
Who's there?
Midas.
Midas who?
Midas well open the door because I'm not going away.

Knock, Knock.
Who's there?
Census.
Census who?
Census Saturday we don't have to go to school.

Knock, Knock.
Who's there?
Trigger.
Trigger who?

Knock, Knock.
Who's there?
Alex.
Alex who?
Alex the questions, if you don't mind.

Knock, Knock.
Who's there?
Formosa.
Formosa who?
Formosa the summer I was away at camp.

Knock, Knock.
Who's there?
Wyoming.
Wyoming who?
Wyoming? Why not?

Knock, Knock.
Who's there?
Zombies.
Zombies who?
Zombies are queens and zombies are drones, and zombies make honey.

Knock, Knock.
Who's there?
Butter.
Butter who?
Butter be quick, I have to go to the bathroom.

Knock, Knock.
Who's there?
Gorilla.
Gorilla who?
Gorilla cheese sandwich for me and I'll be right over.

Knock, Knock.
Who's there?
Cynthia.
Cynthia who?

Knock, Knock.
Who's there?
Don Juan.
Don Juan who?
Don Juan to stay out here forever.

Knock, Knock.
Who's there?
Lucifer.
Lucifer who?
Lucifer coat and you'll be very unhappy.

Knock, Knock.
Who's there?
Thermos.
Thermos who?
Thermos be a better Knock-Knock joke than this one.

Knock, Knock.
Who's there?
Yukon.
Yukon who?
Yukon say that again.
OK, I will. Knock, Knock.
Who's there?
Yukon.
(Repeat over and over.)

Knock, Knock.
Who's there?
Your pencil.
Your pencil who?
Your pencil fall down if you don't wear a belt or suspenders.

Knock, Knock.
Who's there?
Warren.
Warren who?
Warren Peace is a famous Russian novel.

Knock, Knock.
Who's there?
Izzy.
Izzy who?
Izzy come, izzy go.

Knock, Knock.
Who's there?
Ireland.
Ireland who?
Ireland you some money if you promise to pay me back.

Knock, Knock.
Who's there?
Iona.
Iona who?
Iona doorbell which I can let you have.

Knock, Knock.
Who's there?
Egypt.
Egypt who?
Egypt you when he sold you that broken
doorbell.

Knock, Knock.
Who's there?
Sherbert.
Sherbert who?
Sherbert Reynolds can come to your party?

Knock, Knock.
Who's there?
Unite.
Unite who?
Unite a person, you call him Sir.

Knock, Knock.
Who's there?
Lionel.
Lionel who?

Knock, Knock.
Who's there?
Cargo.
Cargo who?
Cargo better if you fill it with gas.

Knock, Knock.
Who's there?
Arthur.
Arthur who?
Arthurmometer is good for measuring the temperature.

Knock, Knock.
Who's there?
Police.
Police who?
Police open the door, I have to go to the bathroom.

Knock, Knock.
Who's there?
Dishes.
Dishes who?
Dishes your friend Margaret, so open the door.

Knock, Knock.
Who's there?
U-Boat.
U-Boat who?
U-Boat can play with me today.

Knock, Knock.
Who's there?
Carrot.
Carrot who?
Knock, Knock.
Who's there?
Carrot.
Carrot who?
Knock, Knock.
Who's there?
Carrot.
Carrot who?
Knock, Knock.
Who's there?
Orange.
Orange who?
Orange you glad I didn't say carrot?

Knock, Knock.
Who's there?
General Lee.
General Lee who?
General Lee speaking, I don't like to go to big parties.

Knock, Knock.
Who's there?
Radio.
Radio who?
Radio not, here I come.

Knock, Knock.
Who's there?
Manny.
Manny who?
Manny are called, but few are chosen.

Knock, Knock.
Who's there?
Venice.
Venice who?
Venice your mother coming home?

Knock, Knock.
Who's there?
Canine.
Canine who?
Canine, I-12, G-3, Bingo!

Knock, Knock.
Who's there?
Isadore.
Isadore who?
Isadore locked?

Knock, Knock.
Who's there?
Dwayne.
Dwayne who?

Knock, Knock.
Who's there?
Wooden.
Wooden who?
Wooden you like to know.

Knock, Knock.
Who's there?
Canoe.
Canoe who?
Canoe come out and play with me?

Knock, Knock.
Who's there?
Aida.
Aida who?
Aida big breakfast before going to school.

Knock, Knock.
Who's there?
Matthew.
Matthew who?
Matthewlaces are untied.

Knock, Knock.
Who's there?
Denial.
Denial who?
Denial's in Egypt, but I'm here.

Knock, Knock.
Who's there?
Closure.
Closure who?
Closure mouth, I'm talking.

Knock, Knock.
Who's there?
Who.
Who who?

Knock, Knock.
Who's there?
Ivan.
Ivan who?
Ivanhoe, by Sir Walter Scott.

Knock, Knock.
Who's there?
Weavish.
Weavish who?
Weavish you a Merry Christmas and a Happy New Year.

Knock, Knock.
Who's there?
Amos.
Amos who?
Amosquito bit me.

Knock, Knock.
Who's there?
Andy.
Andy who?
Andy bit me again.

Knock, Knock.
Who's there?
Pasture.
Pasture who?
Pasture bedtime, isn't it?

Knock, Knock.
Who's there?
Orange juice.
Orange juice who?
Orange juice sorry you asked?

Knock, Knock.
Who's there?
Adore.
Adore who?
Adore stands between us, so open up.

Knock, Knock.
Who's there?
Boo.
Boo who?

Knock, Knock.
Who's there?
Tomorr.
Tomorr who?
You can't even say it right. It's tomorrow, not tomorr who.

Knock, Knock.
Who's there?
Max.
Max who?
Max no difference, just open the door.

Knock, Knock.
Who's there?
Cantaloupe.
Cantaloupe who?
Cantaloupe with you tonight.

Knock, Knock.
Who's there?
Auto.
Auto who?
Auto know, I've forgotten my name.

Knock, Knock.
Who's there?
Weevil.
Weevil who?
Weevil only be staying a minute.

Knock, Knock.
Who's there?
Utah.
Utah who?
Utah the road and I'll mend the fence.

Knock, Knock.
Who's there?
Stan.
Stan who?

Knock, Knock.
Who's there?
Sofa.
Sofa who?
Sofa so good.

Knock, Knock.
Who's there?
Myope.
Myope who?
Myope is that you get well soon.

Knock, Knock.
Who's there?
Tish.
Tish who?
Tishue is good for blowing your nose.

Knock, Knock.
Who's there?
Avon.
Avon who?
Avon lady. I rang the bell, but I guess you didn't hear me.

Knock, Knock.
Who's there?
Knock, Knock.
Who's there?
Knock, Knock.
Who's there?
Knock, Knock.
Who's there?
I'm sorry, but my mother doesn't allow me to speak to strangers.

Knock, Knock.
Who's there?
Lois.
Lois who?

Knock, Knock.
Who's there?
Seymour.
Seymour who?
Seymour if you look out the window.

Knock, Knock.
Who's there?
Tamara.
Tamara who?
Tamara is Tuesday; today is Monday.

Knock, Knock.
Who's there?
Althea.
Althea who?
Althea later in the afternoon.

Knock, Knock.
Who's there?
Atlas.
Atlas who?
Atlas it's Friday and school is out.

Knock, Knock.
Who's there?
Island.
Island who?
Island on your roof with my parachute.

Knock, Knock.
Who's there?
Ivory.
Ivory who?
Ivory strong; how strong are you?

Knock, Knock.
Who's there?
Dewey.
Dewey who?

Knock, Knock.
Who's there?
Socket.
Socket who?
Socket to me.

Knock, Knock.
Who's there?
Oswald.
Oswald who?
Oswald my gum.

Knock, Knock.
Who's there?
Gopher.
Gopher who?
Gopher your gun, Sheriff.

Knock, Knock.
Who's there?
Esau.
Esau who?
Esau me break the window so let me in quick.

Knock, Knock.
Who's there?
Doris.
Doris who?
Doris slammed on my finger so open it quick.

Knock, Knock.
Who's there?
Mica.
Mica who?
Mica is double-parked, so hurry up.

Knock, Knock.
Who's there?
Kansas.
Kansas who?
Kansas come out to play?

Knock, Knock.
Who's there?
Cameron.
Cameron who?
Cameron film are needed to take pictures.

Knock, Knock.
Who's there?
A Fred.
A Fred who?
Who's a Fred of the Big Bad Wolf?

Knock, Knock.
Who's there?
Arthur.
Arthur who?

Knock, Knock.
Who's there?
Dozen.
Dozen who?
Dozen anyone want to let me in?

Knock, Knock.
Who's there?
Tarzan.
Tarzan who?
Tarzan Stripes Forever.

Knock, Knock.
Who's there?
Irish.
Irish who?
Irish you would come outside to play with me.

Knock, Knock.
Who's there?
Odel-Lay-He.
Odel-Lay-He who?

Knock, Knock.
Who's there?
Tennis.
Tennis who?
Tennis the sum of five plus five.

Knock, Knock.
Who's there?
I don't know.
I don't know who?
I told you I don't know. Why don't you believe me?

Knock, Knock.
Who's there?
Spectre.
Spectre who?
Spectre Columbo. You're under arrest.

Knock, Knock.
Who's there?
Sarah.
Sarah who?
Sarah doctor in the house?

Knock, Knock.
Who's there?
Anita.
Anita who?
Anita you like I need a hole in the head.

Knock, Knock.
Who's there?
Nantucket.
Nantucket who?
Nantucket, but she'll give it back.

Knock, Knock.
Who's there?
Elephant.
Elephant who?
Elephantasizes about being a Hollywood star.

Knock, Knock.
Who's there?
Bless.
Bless who?
Did you sneeze?

Knock, Knock.
Who's there?
Halibut.
Halibut who?
Halibut letting me in on the secret?

Knock, Knock.
Who's there?
Sherwood.
Sherwood who?
Sherwood like to meet you.

Knock, Knock.
Who's there?
Tank.
Tank who?
Tank you.

Knock, Knock.
Who's there?
Ammonia.
Ammonia who?
Ammonia gonna tell you once.

Knock, Knock.
Who's there?
Tuna.
Tuna who?
Tuna violin and it will play better.

Knock, Knock.
Who's there?
Pudding.
Pudding who?
Pudding on your shoes before your pants is a bad idea.

Knock, Knock.
Who's there?
Butcher.
Butcher who?
Butcher arms around me.

Knock, Knock.
Who's there?
Dishes.
Dishes who?